Hey, Stop!

Story by Alison Hawes
Illustrated by Sophia Touliatou